AF797158

ABOUT THE AUTHOR

Garth Cameron was admitted to the bar as a Barrister & Solicitor of the High Court of New Zealand in 1980. He has practiced law for 38 years.

HOW TO BE A LAWYER

(THINGS THEY DONT TEACH YOU AT LAW SCHOOL)

Garth Cameron

RainShadow Press

RainShadow Press
P O Box 5441
Dunedin 9058
NEW ZEALAND

garth@garthcameronlaw.co.nz

++ 64 27 622 8428

Copyright©Garth Cameron 2018

Epub ISBN 978-0-473-43105-1
Softcover ISBN 978-0-473-43104-4

Acknowledgements

im Guest, Sue Cheer, Nigel Cameron & Kit McCready provided valuable help.

Contents

INTRODUCTION

The law has become the profession of choice for many bright young people, yet new lawyers are often ill-equipped to enter practice.

Sadly, a big chunk of what is taught at law school is irrelevant to the practice of law. The content of law school courses is law at the appellate level. In practice, most of the lawyering is about facts and personalities. At the appellate level, the facts have usually been decided, and the personalities of the parties are no longer relevant. Lawyers leave law school knowing a lot of law, but little about the skills that lawyering requires. In day-to-day practice, the law is clear, and the issues are factual and personal.

John F. Kennedy appointed his brother, Bobby, Attorney General of the United States and was criticized because his brother had no experience practising law. In fact, the job was the one job a bright new graduate was suited for, using his knowledge of pure law in the upper reaches of government.

I admire straight A students, although I was not one of them. But a grade at law school does not necessarily reflect the potential for good lawyering in practice. There is no reason any student who leaves law school with a reasonable grasp of the law cannot become a good lawyer in the day-to-day practice of law, but they have to re-orient themselves. The change is from a legal theory orientation to a practical orientation.

In legal practice, the facts and personalities are of immense importance, and this book is mostly about resolving disputes of fact and dealing with difficult people.

The advice and examples in this book should make you a better lawyer, sooner.

This is a book that contains the gritty reality of the professional life of lawyers who work in an often-hostile environment, sometimes with clients who will not help their lawyer to help them.

I learnt that the fundamentals of good lawyering are universal across time and space, and this book represents my attempt to explain them using real-world examples.

HOW TO BE A LAWYER

I have been a trial lawyer for 38 years; the observations and anecdotes in this book have been derived from my experiences in court, and in preparation for trial. There are many other types of legal practice, each with its own difficulties and satisfactions. I have tried to make my suggestions as general as possible, but there is an obvious bias toward trial preparation and process.

Trial lawyers represent clients, not because the clients are squeaky clean, but because it is the right of every person in a free society to have their case put in the most effective manner in negotiations and in court. Moreover, "bad" people can nevertheless be innocent and/or have a weak case put up against them.

There are 'perfect' clients with undeniably righteous causes, but it is more common to encounter cases where the rights and wrongs are murky.

The cases I mention have two things in common: none of them is famous, but all of them were important to the clients involved.

If you are looking for a book about white knights defending flawless men and women, you must look elsewhere. If you wish to understand the daily grind of day-to-day trial lawyering, then read on.

The identities of the people who populate these pages have been disguised to protect the virtuous, and the wicked. There are no names, dates or places and some stories have been modified to further protect identities.

NOTE FOR THE GENERAL READER

Lawyers collectively are referred to as the Bar while the body of Judges is referred to as the Bench. In sensible jurisdictions, all lawyers are called attorneys and may do any type of legal work, if they have the skills. In more traditional jurisdictions the legal profession is divided into barristers who do mainly court work and solicitors who do mainly office work. In my jurisdiction, all lawyers are barristers and solicitors although a proportion of lawyers choose to limit themselves to barrister's work. A court may be the place that cases are heard in or a reference to the Judge or Judges, as in 'the Court decided'. Criminal trials may be Judge alone or Judge and Jury with the Judge managing the trial and deciding the law and the Jury deciding factual issues and returning guilty or not guilty verdicts.

CHAPTER 1: THE STAINS LOOKED CURIOUSLY UN-BLOOD LIKE

One day, I was in a colleague's law library, a room lined with volumes of the law reports, each bound identically, each with the year and volume number on the spine. I noticed that a volume from the late nineteen-fifties had a stain on its leather spine, then I noticed that six volumes, in consecutive years, had the same stain. They appeared to have been splashed with a fluid that had faded almost completely away. There were small gashes within the stained areas. I took one of the volumes down and used a letter opener to poke around in one of the gashes, I found small pieces of charred metal and plastic. The stains were blood-stains. The library was in a practice that had been set up in the mid-nineteen-seventies and part of the library had been bought from the firm of a practitioner who had ceased to practice many years before.

One day about thirty years before my discovery of the damaged books, a parcel arrived in the office of a respected general practitioner. His secretary started to unwrap the parcel but stopped when she saw that it was marked personal and confidential. She went into the lawyer's office, put it on his desk, and went back to reception. About a minute later, there was an explosion which blew out all the windows and doors, fatally injuring the lawyer, and spattering his blood and spraying shrapnel across the spines of the law reports.

The murder remains unsolved. Since we do not know who made the bomb, we will never know the motive. Was it for personal reasons, or had the lawyer alienated someone in his capacity as a lawyer? Was it an aggrieved client, or a client on the other side of a dispute? The murderer is probably dead by now. If he is alive, he will take his secret to the grave, for bombers and poisoners never confess.

You are unlikely to receive a bomb in the post, but sometimes you will have to interact with people who have a negative view of lawyers. All lawyers experience tense moments in the office and courtroom and some of them may seem bizarre to non-lawyers. I had a criminal client threaten to assault the prosecutor in the courtroom, immediately after being convicted of an assault. Another would-be client took exception to my request for a modest fee to cover the first consultation and became aggressive. I decided not to reward aggression and showed him to the door, shook his hand, wished him good luck and closed and locked the door. He shouted and ranted for a few minutes, shouting that I was not as good as I thought I was, and left, never to be seen again. Clients who feel deeply insecure sometimes become aggressive when they believe that the lawyer is being arrogant or talking down to them. All you can do is to be calm, ride out the anger and get them out the door.

A colleague represented an overseas client who was in the country to do some business. One day he turned up in the colleague's office with his minder, a Neanderthal with hideous tattoos a powerful build and a fierce look. There was no perceptible reason why the client had to bring him to a routine conference. A few weeks later the client left the country suddenly and for no obvious reason. A few weeks after that, before my colleague finalized the transaction, he received a visit at home from a stranger, tall and powerfully built with many visible tattoos and a large dog on a leash. The stranger did not introduce himself or give a reason for the visit. What he did do was take the dog off the leash and explain that the dog was a killer but only when told to. He then put the dog back on the leash and left. Our best guess was that the client arranged the visits as intimidation and a warning that bad things would happen if he was dissatisfied with the legal services.

There is not much you can do about bombs and attack dogs except doing good work and be ethical, honest and diligent.

The good news is that there are many practices instituted by the profession that has helped to change the image of lawyers and recent surveys show that lawyers now have a positive image. In part, this may be because the profession goes to a great deal of trouble to explain to clients what they can and can't do for them. In addition, there is an emphasis on keeping the clients up to date. This is to avoid a situation where the case is progressing, but the client is worried because he or she has not received regular reports on that progress.

Lawyering is one of the most interesting and responsible jobs on the planet. Lawyers have the duty to ask all the important and interesting questions and insist on answers.

You will meet people you would otherwise never met and hear their stories, which are sometimes stranger than fiction. In pursuit of a good result for your clients, you will be challenged in ways you never imagined.

I sometimes think lawyers are more critical of their profession than the public. Part of the reason is that law is competitive and knocking a fellow lawyer may be a business strategy. Sometimes this leads to on-going trouble between law firms. There was a small city in which two law firms became highly adversarial and the other firms were drawn in. This is bad for many reasons, the most important being that a war between law firms does not assist the client. Your client's cause is best served by having a lawyer who has a good working relationship with the lawyers on the other side. It also leads to unnecessary stress and non-productive time. If I sense a build-up of animosity between my firm and another firm I talk to one of their senior partners and try and smooth things over.

There will be times when a client will ask you for an opinion on the quality of another lawyer's work and you must do so. Make sure you have read the file before you give your opinion. Remember that your first duty is to the client, but you must be dispassionate and measured, rather than aggressive and judgmental. If you are about to criticize a colleague, remember that he or she will always hear about it and, at the right time, can and will criticize you.

CHAPTER 2: THE BIG PICTURE

If you watch the evening news you will frequently view items about democracies which are democratic in name only. Their democratic institutions have usually been progressively eroded because few people have the will or courage to challenge the government. Several institutions must work together to maintain real democracy and one of them is a strong and fearless legal profession, a strong and independent judiciary is another. Your duties include helping to maintain the rule of law.

All governments wish to govern as simply and effectively as possible and lawyers stand in the way of this by fighting for the rights of the individual. All governments lie or at least mislead the electorate and when they increase their power they misrepresent it and claim that the changes are necessary and there are built-in safeguards. The changes are often to make arrest, search, seizure and surveillance easier and more pervasive. Their position is something like, 'trust us with your civil liberties', when in fact without the judiciary and the lawyers they will inevitably misuse these powers. Even benign governments lose their way and need to be reminded that basic human rights should not be reduced by law changes that seem necessary but may not be.

Most of you will never do a major constitutional law case but you can fight for the average citizen in small but important ways. Every time you act as defence counsel in a criminal case you are ensuring that the client's rights are protected and keeping the police honest. Advising clients before and during a police interview, challenging the admissibility of evidence obtained unlawfully, cross-examining prosecution witnesses and generally making the prosecution prove its case beyond reasonable doubt serve to maintain the rule of law and fundamental human rights.

I have done between 2,500 and 3,000 criminal cases all of which have these things in common; none of them were major, all of them were important to the client and collectively they were a contribution to the preservation of democratic institutions.

It is your duty to take on cases that may seem unwinnable, and that requires you to take on Big Business and Big Government. You will find that, if you have moral courage and if the right is on your side, you can take on city hall and can win.

When you read about proposed law changes which reduce civil rights you should lobby the politicians to maintain or improve the status quo.

You can and should make a difference.

CHAPTER 3: QUALITIES AND SKILLS

John Mortimer QC, an English Barrister and author of the 'Rumpole of the Bailey' novels, received some advice from his father, who was also a Barrister and was the author of a standard legal textbook. Mortimer Senior said that all that was required was common sense and clean fingernails. Mortimer Junior has written that additional skills are an understanding of law and procedure, and the ability to look up what you don't know.

Here are some other skills you need.

Honesty and integrity are givens. If you don't have them, you should not be contemplating practising law.

Moral courage is just as important but is more difficult to understand. If you are doing criminal law, you must be prepared to represent someone who is despised by the community, and you must do your best for that person, whatever your own beliefs and feelings. You must be prepared to decline instructions that require you to behave unethically, despite the obvious displeasure of your client, and the risk that the client will sack you. Never do something unethical just to obtain a momentary advantage for a client who does not care what happens to you.

Be prepared to tell your client something that they don't want to hear. If their case has no foundation in law or fact, you must tell them so. Do it right, and often they will respect you for it. There may be better follow-on business from that client.

Be objective. Give the client what they don't have – a clear perspective on the problem. Care about your client and seek a good outcome, but do not lose your detachment.

Learn to take a comprehensive history from the client. Clients have a natural but unhelpful tendency to cherry pick facts. Be prepared to winkle out information that you must have, but which the client is reluctant to give you because it does not help their cause.

Instructions from the client are received in two, equally important stages. When you take a history from a client you are taking instructions consisting of what the client tells you about the facts, the problem, and the desired outcome. After advising the client on what their options are, the client will give you instructions as to what they want you to do. If the client will not give you clear instructions at either or both stages, you must not do anything. An instruction to do what you think is best is worse than useless and should not be acted upon.

Clear instructions, in writing and signed correctly by the client, must be obtained before you do anything. A firm agreement on the fee must be reached at the same time.

Keep files that record all relevant information. Get the client to check your notes and sign them. If the case is complex, write a letter to the client setting out, in plain English, all relevant information. The file will show that you are acting competently and in a timely manner and will protect you against complaints.

You must have a theory of the case for every client. For example, if it is a murder, it might be that the client used reasonable force in defending himself. In a civil case involving a road accident, it might be that the other driver was careless, crossed the centreline of the road, and caused the damage to your client's car.

You must have a system that reminds you of key dates, such as, the date by which some document must be filed in court and served on the other party.

Good communication skills, both spoken and written, are essential. Learn to express yourself so clearly that you cannot be misunderstood. Always use plain English. Imagine that some lawyer will try to twist your words to the advantage of his or her client. Write as if the letter, email, document, or file note will be read by a judge who does not like you. You are preventing misrepresentation of what you have said.

Keep looking for creative ways to resolve problems, one that will satisfy both sides.

Never encourage clients to seek revenge, or dwell on an old grievance, or pursue a claim that has little chance of success. In fact, actively discourage them.

I was approached by a man who had operated a trucking business and required an operating certificate to be issued by the state. This was withdrawn, and he had to close his business. He appealed the decision, and there was a two-day trial, which he lost. He discussed a further appeal with his lawyer and opted to take the matter no further. This happened seven years before he came to see me. I took a detailed history and confirmed that nothing could be done to put things right. I advised him to go home, burn the files, take his wife out to dinner, and get on with his life.

A divorce may be followed by bitter disputes (or indeed also be preceded by them). I came across one in the law reports, where the property at issue was valued at $1,200,000 (a lot of money at the time). The case had gone on appeal several times, and the latest appeal kept the case alive. The husband and wife had spent $550,000 on the litigation. They had allowed bitterness to consume a big chunk of the property, and there was no end in sight. This behaviour is surprisingly common.

Always explain litigation risk – the risk that their claim will fail, and they will be worse off than if they did nothing. A client sued an insurance company because they declined his claim. The company offered a settlement. The client rejected the offer, went to trial, lost, and had to pay his fees, the company's fees, and failed to recover any money. A bird in the hand may be better than two in the bush, as the old saying goes.

Every day of that you practice law will require you to be ethical, exercise moral courage, and manage your client's expectations of what you can do for him or her. You will never stop learning and will seldom be bored.

CHAPTER 4: FIFTEEN MYTHS ABOUT THE PRACTICE OF LAW

There are many myths about the practice of law and these are some of them:

Law schools train lawyers.

In fact, they teach the law. Much of what you learn in law school will never be used by you, whose practice consists of day-to-day problem-solving. The law degree is still a great academic degree, but it is not an apprenticeship for lawyers.

When you leave law school you have the knowledge and skills to successfully practice law.

No. You still have a lot to learn, but learning is a positive experience and will continue throughout your entire career.

A straight-A student will always be a better lawyer than one who gets straight Cs.

In the day-to-day practice of law, the C student may be a better lawyer. All new lawyers, irrespective of their grades in law school, need to adapt to the day-to-day challenges of practising law. Each of you will bring different personal or innate skills; other skills can be learned.

Thinking like a lawyer is thinking like a law professor.

In fact, it is thinking about facts, and personalities, and what result would be acceptable to both sides, against a background your knowledge of the law.

The practice of law is about applying your knowledge of the law to the client's problems.

A lawyer must know enough law to recognize legal issues, but problem-solving is almost always fact-based and/or process-based.

Your client is always right.

Frequently, the client is wrong, or at least confused. The client is too close to the problem to be able to assess it objectively. It is your job to clarify matters for him or her. Most clients are reasonable if they think they can trust you, and that you are on their side.

A client always knows what his problem is, and the outcome he wants.

Clients often cannot define the problem and sometimes do not know exactly what result they want. It is your role to talk things through, help your client define the problem, and understand his or her options to solve the problem.

A client will always help his lawyer to help him.

No. Often the lawyer must persuade his client to do things like keeping appointments, supplying documents, not breaching bail and generally not doing anything that will compromise their case. The client and lawyer must work as a team. Explain this point, and usually, the client will see the value of the team approach to problem-solving.

A lawyer must do whatever his client tells him to do.

A lawyer is not a neutral conduit or a mouthpiece. The lawyer must not carry out an instruction to do something unethical or unlawful. If the instructions are simply unwise, advise the client against that course of action. You owe it to your client to be firm.

A lawyer should be uncompromising.

Compromise is the way to swiftly resolve your client's problems.

A lawyer should always advise a client to do something.

A rather crusty old lawyer once said, 'half the practice of a good lawyer is to tell the client that he is being a damn fool and should stop'. Although it is not half the practice, it is a situation that you will encounter from time-to-time. Convincing a client that the best thing to do is nothing, is a challenge.

A long, detailed contract, with all the advantage to your client, is always the best way to assist your client.

No. This is a recipe for disaster. It is better to negotiate a contract that is fair to both sides because both sides will be motivated to honour it. A short, clear, contract is usually best, as it is easy to interpret.

The cost of going to a lawyer to solve your problem is the lawyer's fee.

Cost includes more than just the lawyer's fee and can be assessed in terms other than those that are monetary. The true cost includes stress, wasted time, and lost opportunities to move on and do something positive.

A court is the best place to resolve a dispute.

It is almost always quicker and cheaper to resolve things informally. Discuss and negotiate with the other side. That is why the so-called Alternative Dispute Resolution techniques of mediation, conciliation, and arbitration have become so widely used.

If you recognize that a negotiated settlement is not possible, the client has the options of giving up or going to court.

A good lawyer, with a vast experience of the practice of the law, will always make a good judge.

The skills required for good lawyering are not the same as for good judging. For example, lawyers are paid to talk, whereas judges are paid to listen.

CHAPTER 5: MISSION STATEMENT

You need to decide what you want from the practice of law and to plan how to achieve these goals. You do this by creating a mission statement.

A mission statement is like a theory of the case., In both instances, the purpose is to decide what you want, and how to get it. Every step you take is intended to attain that goal.

The best way to explain this is to summarize my aims at various stages of my career:

Before starting law school. I wanted to obtain a law degree, pass postgraduate qualifications, and to be admitted to the Bar. I did not strive to be a straight-A student, as I wanted to participate in some time consuming extra-curricular activities. I should have also tried to find part-time work in a law office so that I could put my legal studies in a practical context.

Going to work for my first firm I wanted to learn as much as I could about as many areas of practice as possible and to observe and learn practical skills from experienced lawyers in the office, and the courtroom. I wanted to build a personal knowledge base. My aim was essentially to immerse myself in my chosen profession and to be satisfied with a living wage while I did so.

When offered a partnership or profit share it was important to consider the pros and cons of accepting the offer, and whether I wanted to go on being a team player. After working for two firms for a total of three-and-a-half years, I decided that I would be happier setting up my own firm.

Setting up my own firm, I had several goals, to accept instructions in many types of law, but build up experience and expertise in civil and criminal litigation, and specialise in these areas as soon I felt able. To be scrupulously honest and ethical, and never stop learning. To have low overheads and no bad debts. To earn more than I was earning as an employee, but not try to get rich. To practice in a way that allowed a good work-life balance.

At least once a year I re-consider my professional and personal goals and modify my practice accordingly. I am committed to continuing learning new ways to achieve more in each area. I ask myself: 'why am I practising law, and what do I hope to achieve'?

CHAPTER 6: AS RARE AS A UNICORN

A client comes to see you. He clearly explains the problem and listens carefully to your advice, and then gives you instructions that are clear and reasonable. The facts are clearly favourable to your client's cause. You research the law and find what you are after. The lawyer for the other side accepts that his client cannot win, and the case is speedily resolved in your client's favour. You render a modest bill. The client pays promptly, phones to tell you how pleased he is, and speaks well of you to potential clients. Such clients are rare, a cynic would say; as rare as a unicorn.

A more likely scenario is that a client arrives in the office upset and confused, without a clear idea of the problem, or what he or she wants to achieve. Your job is to take a history and help the client to define the problem. I encourage the client to talk part of the time and listen part of the time. I tell the client that, once the basis of the problem has been identified, I ask a series of questions. This usually causes the interview to move forward meaningfully and reasonably quickly. When I think I understand the problem, I go back over my notes and ask the client if I have covered everything he or she thinks is important, and then ask them to tell me if I have missed anything.

I then outline all the options open to the client and discuss them, so that the client can make an informed decision.

I have already quoted a fee for the first consultation and try to advise the client about the fees and disbursements he or she is likely to incur with each option. This is simple for a well-defined problem, such as a careless driving charge and difficult for a complex civil case. In the former case, I can quote a fee for a trial, or for a guilty plea. In the latter case, I explain that there are too many variables to quote an all-in fee but will quote an hourly rate and suggest that progress is reviewed at regular intervals so that the client can decide if the fees are well spent. No client likes paying fees but is most likely to accept them if you invoice regularly so that he or she always knows what the process is costing. I usually ask that fees are paid into my office before the work is done. If you are communicating well and gain the client's trust, he or she will listen, will consider advice, and give you instructions which are reasonable.

If the client knows that you understand the problem, care about them and about results, stick to the fees discussed, and achieve a result within the range you told them, it is likely that they will see your service as being value for money.

Regularly, but not frequently, a client from hell seeks you out. He or she comes to your office angry and frustrated. They do not have a clear idea of what the problem is, or the result they want. He or she does not listen and wants you to do something that is unethical and/or illegal. The client reluctantly agrees to pay a fee but does not want to pay until they see a positive outcome. The law is clear, but the facts are not, and the client refuses to understand the difference between what he or she believes, and what can be proven. You carefully tease out the issues, and what the client wants. They give you instructions that are unclear, and difficult to carry out. You have quoted a fee for this first consultation, they do not want to pay it because they only wanted advice and does not see the value in the advice.

The client knows he or she must make appointments to see his or her dentist or accountant but turns up in your office without one 'just to see how his case is going'. They are displeased when you are not available. They send emails and expect instant answers, even after hours. Their constant unnecessary communications increase the time engaged, and they complain about a number of your bills.

The client instructs you settle the case, but is unhappy with the outcome and is slow to pay your fees. He or she goes off and badmouths you all over town.

The lessons are that the law is usually clear, and the facts are what results in a success or a failure. Clients tend to be difficult to manage, and their expectations can be excessive. Many clients don't want to pay, even when they win; the most difficult part of legal practice is getting paid.

The good news is that most clients will co-operate most of the time when they see that it is the quickest and least expensive way to a result.

A thoroughly professional and client-centred approach will usually result in a satisfied client.

CHAPTER 7: MORE ABOUT CLIENTS

To cross a desert, you must understand the terrain and its challenges. To cross an ocean, you must understand its swells, waves, and storms. The most important part of the legal landscape are the clients, with their multifarious problems, requirements, demands, and quirks. Some personality traits make people difficult to work with. These people tend to think they know everything about everything or are unpleasant or find it difficult to make up their minds. In addition, some occupations tend to generate particularly difficult clients; you will soon work out which vocations they are.

Some clients are obnoxious and impossible to please. I was assigned to a client on legal aid. He rang up the day I was assigned and was unpleasant because I had not moved his case forward. He instructed me to refrain from discussing the case with the lawyers for the other two defendants. He demanded that property seized under a search warrant be returned (before the trial). He expected me to be available at any time of the day or night. He acted as if he was in a strong position, despite the evidence against him being overwhelming and tried to manipulate the system. After the case was over he tried to block payment of my invoice, out of pure malice (he was not paying the legal fees).

People in business can be difficult, because they don't want to be pinned down to one set of instructions, and they change their instruction at frequent intervals. They are used to operating with changing goal posts and they treat their case the same way. They are fee resistant, want to pay for a result instead of a service, and not at all if they don't get what they want. I have always found it simpler to act for criminals: the issues tend to be clear, the instructions are straightforward, the case has a clear beginning, middle and end, and the most difficult ones are locked up where they can't bother you.

I recall a university lecturer who bought numerous books from a shop and charged them all to his account. The manager phoned him and politely reminded him that he had not paid any of the invoices for five years. The lecturer made it clear that he was offended. After all, he had been buying books for five years. He was pompous and was miffed when the manager pointed out that he had uplifted the books and had not bought them until he had paid. Academics go from school to university, to teaching postings, and are not exposed to the commercial realities of day-to-day life. I have found academics to be charming and knowledgeable, but sometimes reluctant to accept that a lawyer knows more about legal issues than they do.

Any client who will not give clear instructions, or changes them at frequent intervals, is prima facie difficult. Difficulty in obtaining clear instructions is a major source of stress for lawyers and reduces the opportunities for a good result that the client will not recognise as a positive outcome.

Some people go through life shouting, bullying and generally being obnoxious. They have gotten away with it all their lives and have no intention of being polite in your office. Often, they will be angry, insist on ranting, and won't listen. This type of client doesn't realize that such behaviour reduces the quality of service that can be provided. A lawyer preoccupied with handling such a client may not discover a fact that would help to get the result the client wants. Composed clients get better service, and it is often the professionalism of the lawyer that gets them composed.

Some clients are used to subterfuge or lying to get the results they want. With experience, you will develop a sense that something is off. A man came to see me and told me that he had been sentenced to three months' imprisonment for breaching a restraining order, and all he had done was write to his wife and wish her well. I knew that he was not telling me everything. When I looked at his criminal record sheet, I found that he had neglected to tell me that the breach was his sixteenth. I acted for him for a month or so and found that he was a man whose word was not to be trusted, on any subject. It is your duty to act for people you would rather not act for.

A client stormed into my office and told me that a friend had told him, that his (the client's) case was easy and should have been resolved long ago. I persuaded him that his friend was wrong. All lawyers encounter clients who have been given misleading advice from friends and acquaintances. The friends are not lawyers, don't understand the client's case, wish to appear knowledgeable, and tell the client what he or she wants to hear – mostly that the case should be sorted out quickly and cheaply. The client may think the lawyer is not acting competently. The lawyer then must spend time re-earning the client's trust.

Important clients can make bad lawyers. You want to keep their business, and it is tempting to tell them what they want to hear. It is far better to tell them what you would tell any client. If you are going to practice law, you will have to interact with difficult people. You will also have to decide, on a case-by-case basis, whether the game is worth the candle. Some clients are more trouble than they are worth but achieving a satisfactory result for difficult clients can be personally rewarding.

You must not judge your clients – that is for the judges and the courts. You must do your best for them, within the limits set out in the ethical rules.

You will be relieved to hear that some of your clients will be charming, interesting, and will do everything possible to help you to help them. Those clients have recognized that a case is a co-operative effort, in which lawyer and client work together to obtain a good outcome.

CHAPTER 8: SELF REPRESENTATION

There are people who choose to be their own lawyers. Sometimes, they do it because they believe that they are the only person who understands the importance and merit of their cause, or it may be that legal services are perceived as expensive and their value may not be recognised.

Sometimes you will find yourself representing a client in a case where the other party does not have a lawyer and insists on representing himself or herself. They have never heard that "a person who acts as his own lawyer has a fool for a client."

Self-represented parties call for special handling because they are not objective, do not have the skills to assess the merits of their case, and don't understand the lawyering process. They don't have to obey any code of ethics, and don't understand how to "get to yes". Encourage them to seek representation, even if it is only advice, at key moments in the process.

I always record phone conversations and interviews with self- represented people (after telling them that I am going to do it). This ensures that they cannot misrepresent what has been said. I insist that all proposals be made in writing. Not all my colleagues agree with me on this point. Perhaps the best policy is to adopt my suggestion if you think that the self-represented person is a bit slippery.

Sometimes, my client wants to do most of his or her legal work. They do that because they want to save money. These clients need to be treated with caution. They want to ring up from time-to-time and get prompt, cheap, advice. The client/lawyer relationship is a fertile field for misunderstandings and dissatisfaction on the part of the client. I explain that the savings on legal fees may be illusory. Every time I am instructed to advise or to act, I must spend time reviewing the steps the client has taken. It may take no more time for me to do all the work, and there is always a better chance of a good result if I do the work, and the client co-operates in the lawyering exercise.

It is better to lose the client than do a half-baked job and risk major client dissatisfaction.

CHAPTER 9: ADVOCACY AND THE BEST POINT

A friend of mine was a good lawyer and became a respected judge. He was certain that a lawyer was only as good as his best point. The best point is a provable fact or relevant piece of law that gives a tangible prospect of victory.

I have confessed to knowing little about how to be a lawyer when I started out. Despite my inexperience, I won my first criminal judge-alone trial, first criminal jury trial, first criminal appeal, first family trial, and first family appeal. My first civil trial was successful. I acted in cases against two very able and experienced lawyers and won both. I was inexperienced but able to identify the facts and law that resulted in good results. I won these cases despite my inexperience and lack of skill. I won because the merits were on the side of my client, and all I had to do was make sure they were presented to the best advantage.

If none of the facts and/or the law are favourable to your cause, you usually lose but chance is always a factor, for example, your opponent makes a real mess of it or his or her witnesse(s) fail to turn up or don't provide evidence of some essential fact.

If you have a slender but arguable point, experience and skill may make the difference between winning and losing.

To wage war in the office and courtroom you must be able to identify the point or points with which you can attain a good outcome. Advocacy is making the most of those favourable facts and law by presenting them in the most persuasive way. Great advocates are made but you can become a good advocate by study and constant practice. Learn from experienced lawyers, note effective techniques and learn from the mistakes of your colleagues. Read books by and about leading advocates, attend litigation skills seminars and keep notebooks. Advertising is advocacy and it is instructive to assess the reasons why advertisements work or don't work.

Every lawyer is an advocate, even those who never go to court. Each letter, email, court document or conversation with the other parties' lawyer is a piece of advocacy that is intended to advance your client's cause.

Plain English is an effective tool in advocacy, whether it be written or spoken.

Advocacy is challenging, and successful advocacy is deeply satisfying. Advocacy is the tool with which you optimize your client's prospects of success.

CHAPTER 10: JUDGES

Judges and judging are mysteries to many lay people and to some lawyers as well.

In my jurisdiction judges are appointed by the Governor-General, acting on the advice of the Attorney-General, who has consulted with senior members of the judicial system. There are no confirmation hearings and the Attorney-General acts independently of party political considerations. The process is said to be transparent, but it is a little murky, all that is known for sure is the that the judge has more than seven years legal experience, has filled out the application forms and impresses those in the judicial system as competent and honest, as most judges are. Many judges have been prosecutors, and many have strong connections in the Law Society, but few people know what goes on behind closed doors during the selection process.

I don't think there is a perfect way to assess and appoint judges, and the system described above is as good as any other and better than some.

Once a judge is appointed only Parliament can remove him or her, so judges have tenure. Once they are on the bench is almost impossible to take them off it. This is more appropriate than it sounds because judges must be able to fearlessly decide their cases without worrying about arbitrary removal.

If you are a trial lawyer, you must learn how to interact effectively with judges. It is essential that you gain and retain their trust. You may not get on with some judges, but it essential that all of them know that they can trust you.

Judges are human. They have arguments with their spouses and their children. They must buy the groceries and pay the mortgage. My point is that they are human beings first, and judges second.

Many judges are competent and easy to work with. If you are well prepared, they will help you (and your opponent) to move the case forward. These judges remember the pressures and difficulties that you are dealing with at the Bar, and don't blame you for your client's actions.

Sometimes you will encounter judges whose behaviour changed for the worse the moment they were appointed to the Bench. Some of these judges don't enjoy the job and reveal this by constant rudeness. Some do enjoy the job, and the power it gives them to make life difficult for lawyers. Lawyers are paid to talk, and some judges never adapt to the fact that judging is a job that requires a lot of patient listening.

I recall a judge who spent more than 30 years on the Bench and was rude to almost every lawyer who appeared before him. When he retired there was a Bar Dinner to mark the occasion and I decided not to honour a man who had made my professional life unnecessarily difficult. Most of the trial lawyers did attend and did honour him. Why they did so is a mystery to me.

A lawyer forgot to turn his cell-phone off and it rang in court. He immediately stood up, switching the phone off and apologised while he did so, the whole process taking less than 20 seconds. The judge ordered the court orderly to take the phone and give it to the court registrar and directed that it be impounded for three hours. The same judge threatened to fine a lawyer because the lawyer had not filled out a form to the Judge's satisfaction. You may think that the Judge was being stunningly childish, I certainly do.

Some judges are competent most of the time but occasionally get it spectacularly wrong, which is one reason why there is an appeal process. Sadly, not all errors by Judges have a remedy, and the client can only live with the result. Other Judges don't know what to do when presented with novel issues and do nothing. This forces the lawyers to make him resolve the impasse. Other judges are polite but severe, one of whom was nick-named smiling death.

The efficient administration of justice requires that the Bar support the Bench and the Bench support the Bar, something that is sometimes forgotten by the Bench. If the lawyer is polite and respectful and the judge is rude, the support is entirely one way.

If you are always well prepared you will gain the respect and trust of the good judges, and this will help you to help your clients. Being well prepared will give you the confidence to appear and survive in the court of any of the more difficult members of the judiciary.

Treat difficult judges as you treat difficult clients – as a challenge that can be overcome.

CHAPTER 11: LIMITATIONS

There are many things a lawyer can do to help clients but there are limits. A lawyer cannot make inconvenient facts disappear or cause the law to be changed or make an unreasonable person reasonable or an unpleasant experience (e.g. dealing with an ex-spouse) pleasant.

A husband and wife went to see a colleague of mine. Earlier that day, they had met with the husband's oncologist. The husband had been diagnosed with cancer, and the doctor had told them that, no matter what treatment the husband received, he would probably die within the next three months. They felt aggrieved and their first reaction was to consult their lawyer.

There was no suggestion of malpractice, or that better treatment would be obtained with the encouragement of a lawyer's letter. The visit to the lawyer's office was an automatic reaction to hearing the distressing news. My colleague explained this in a tactful way, and the couple went off to deal with the situation as best they could.

Lawyers are no better than any other person in the presence of death, weather, or taxes; although a tax lawyer might disagree with the last proposition.

A lawyer may be an advocate or a witness in Court, he or she cannot be both and this a point that many clients have a problem understanding. This is especially so when the lawyer makes frequent references to the evidence or asserts some fact that has not been proven. He or she can only assert such a fact if it is one that is beyond dispute, such as the time of sunrise on a particular day.

To gain and retain the trust of your clients you must be able to explain the things you can do and the things you can't do, in a clear and memorable way.

CHAPTER 12: THE FIRST THREE YEARS IN THE LAW

Great lawyers are born. Good lawyers are made by hard work and constant study. Not just of the law but, more importantly, the skills required in the day-to-day practice of the law.

Your career starts the moment you arrive at law school, for it is then you start learning and forming important relationships.

In some jurisdictions, as soon as you have qualified you are be entitled to hang up your shingle and get down to it. In others, you must spend time working in a law office before you are permitted to start your own firm.

I advise you to work for an established firm, for a minimum of three years. These are the years that you will learn, or fail to learn, the core skills. They are also the years in which you will start to earn a reputation. It is up to you if that reputation is a positive one.

My first job out of law school was in a five-partner practice in a medium-sized city. I was lucky enough to work for the litigation partner and benefited from learning good practical lessons from his skills in the office, and the courtroom. The partner appears later in this book, dressed in a gorilla suit. One of the important lessons I learnt was that the life of a lawyer does not always have to be deadly serious.

My main work was doing minor criminal cases and all kinds of family law. Invariably the issues were factual – whom should the court believe? and personal – was it possible to negotiate a satisfactory result with an angry man or woman on each side? I also acted in minor civil cases. I did judge-alone trials regularly, and appeals from decisions in criminal, civil, and family cases. Experienced trial lawyers brought me in as junior counsel in their jury trials.

I can do no better than advise you to do what I did. Work hard, listen, keep notebooks. Write down every question and every answer. Do every kind of law your employer engages in.

Observe and learn from other lawyers in the office, and in the courtroom. Even bad lawyers have something to teach you, if only how not to do things. Read every legal memoir, autobiography and biography you can find. Decide what kind of law you want to practice and learn everything you can about it. The first thing that a lawyer must learn is that there is a limit to what they can do for a client. You will spend your entire career thinking about what you can do to advance your clients' causes.

CHAPTER 13: MANAGING STRESS

This topic deserves a book of its own, but some techniques can be explained in a few words. I have found managing stress a challenge but have learnt some valuable methods.

Firstly, don't take on more work than you can handle. I know of good lawyers who did not know how to say no and took on more work that they could handle, promised everything and did nothing. That practice guarantees client dissatisfaction and is certain to result in the stress of disciplinary action and civil action for damages.

There is nothing so stressful as acting for a client who is reluctant to give clear instructions. If you can't see the goal posts, you can't get the ball over them. Insist on clear instructions and stress the benefits of not changing instructions without a very good reason.

Manage client expectations. Explain what you can achieve, may be able to achieve and what you cannot achieve. Develop good working relationships with clients, be sincere, reliable and diligent.

Insist that clients make appointments, and don't respond to phone calls or emails outside of normal working hours. There will be exceptions to these practices. Be flexible, but try to plan your day, and keep your personal time insulated from client demands.

Ensure that the agreed fee is secured in some way (e.g. held in a trust account) before doing any major amount of work.

Recognise when you are not making progress on a file. If you have some kind mental block, talk to the client about it. It is better to suggest a change of lawyer than face an angry client who might sue you because you have done nothing, and consequently lost an opportunity for him or her.

Work out which lawyers are competent and honest and develop strong, mutually supportive relationships with them. Use them as sounding boards and do the same for them. Be prepared to help them when they are busy or sick

All lawyers experience stress-related issues, you must acquire the skills to limit the source of stress and deal with it when it becomes too much for you.

Work out where your happy place is and go there (figuratively or literally) as often as you can.

CHAPTER 14: BUT HE DIDN'T DO ANYTHING

Desperate people sometimes retreat into denial and fantasy, and some of your clients (and their families) will be desperate people. Despite the evidence against them, either they or their families will believe that they did not do what they have been accused of doing.

I was standing in the corridor outside the court where my client had just been sentenced to two years' imprisonment. I was dressed in working rig, horsehair wig, high-collared white shirt with white tapes, black Bar-jacket, black robe, trousers, and shoes.

The Defendant's wife had a vice-like grip on the sleeve of my robe and kept repeating "but he didn't do anything''. But he had. And he had done it before.

About five years earlier, he had driven dangerously and killed a passenger in the car he collided with. On that occasion, he had narrowly avoided a sentence of imprisonment.

This time the facts were that he had driven recklessly, and had collided head-on with a car, killing its elderly driver instantly, and had been charged with manslaughter. The wife knew exactly what he had done because she (and their children) had been in the client's car.

There was no possibility of a not guilty verdict at trial, so he entered a guilty plea, and instructed me to concentrate on persuading the court to impose the minimum possible sentence. He was exposed to a possible sentence of life imprisonment.

The judge imposed a sentence of two years imprisonment and said that the client should never drive again, but, due to a quirk in the law, the longest term of disqualification that could be imposed was three years. The prosecution appealed the sentence, arguing that it was manifestly inadequate, but the appeal court dismissed the appeal.

There is no doubt in my mind that the penalty was inadequate, but my opinion was irrelevant because my job had been to argue the client's case as best I could.

The client was released from prison after one year of his sentence and was back on the road after another two years. I am certain that neither the client or his wife ever thought that the penalty anything other than harsh.

Another client was charged with the burglary of business premises. He had worked there not long before and knew where the cash box was. He sat outside in his car for 45 minutes, and then ran inside, grabbed the cash box, returned to the car, which he then drove off. It was in the middle of the day, and three witnesses had a clear view of what he did. One of the witnesses had worked with him, and all three positively identified him. He came to me, told me he did not commit the crime, had an alibi, and was pleading not guilty. The alibi witness failed to give him an alibi, and the client was unable to account for the positive identifications set out in the prosecution witness statements. Eventually, and with every sign of dissatisfaction, he changed his plea to guilty.

Another client presented a forged document to a parole board, in support an application for early release. When he was charged with fraud, he pleaded not guilty, accepted that the document had been forged, that the original document would not have helped him, and that the forged document assisted him in his application. However, he claimed that a friend had forged it, and he had not noticed the forgery. He changed his plea to guilty after I pointed out that his chances of a not-guilty verdict were close to zero.

CHAPTER 15: SOMETIMES YOU CANNOT SAVE YOUR CLIENTS

A client was facing several charges of aggravated assault. If he was convicted, the court could sentence him to up to seven years' imprisonment. His defence was implausible, but he rejected my advice to plead guilty, and thereby benefit from the reduced sentence that an early guilty is rewarded with. He pleaded not guilty, and a jury trial was set down for hearing.

The first thing I noticed was his shaved head. The tattoo occupying the entire crown of his head was a political symbol of the most offensive kind. Although I advised him to let his hair grow out before the trial, and he agreed to do so, on the day of the trial he arrived with a freshly shaved head. The jury heard all the evidence, retired for a brief period, and convicted him on all charges. I have no doubt that the speed of the jury's decision was influenced by my client's appearance. Letting his hair grow out to cover the tattoo may not have changed the verdict but perhaps his case may have been given more consideration.

In another case, the client was fifty-two-year-old who had devoted much of his adult life to getting "shit faced" (a crude term in some parts of the world for utterly intoxicated) and driving, resulting in numerous court appearances.

He did it one time too many and was facing imprisonment, and the loss of his liquor licence (he owned a bar). He expected his lawyer to perform a plea in mitigation so effective that he would keep his business and his freedom. His blood-alcohol level was astronomical, but the client believed that the doctor who took the blood sample would report that he was not badly affected.

The doctor's report, which was presented to the judge, assessed the client as 'unfit to be a pedestrian'. My client was sentenced to imprisonment, lost his liquor licence, and his livelihood. His wife also left him.

CHAPTER 16: ADVICE

Some clients don't like paying for advice, yet good advice, given early, is priceless. I encourage clients to take advice early, by discounting my fee by 50% for a first consultation. If you give good advice, most clients will see the value in it.

A client's friend had received a phone call from his distressed sister. She was a victim of an ongoing domestic assault by her boyfriend. The brother drove to the scene and confronted the perpetrator. The assault had finished, but the brother stabbed the perpetrator to death. My client had been present and had travelled to the scene in the murderer's car. He had been within feet of the stabbing and had witnessed the whole thing.

The police wanted to interview my client. If he had encouraged the murderer or provided the knife (knowing what would be done with it), he would be guilty of murder as a party.

I met with the client and his father within hours of the killing. I advised the client to decline to make a statement or be interviewed and told him that anything he said to anyone (other than me) could be used against him. My instructions were to keep the client out of court. I informed the police and told them that the client would co-operate if he was given immunity. They declined to do this.

The murder case went to trial, and the accused was found not guilty of murder, but guilty of manslaughter and was sentenced to ten years' imprisonment. My client was never charged.

The client's father said that his son had not even been called as a witness, and paid my invoice with every show of resentment. I think the father had decided his son was never at risk; he could not have been more mistaken. Clients' (and their loved ones') appreciation of good lawyering diminishes rapidly after the crisis has passed.

The optimum moment for a client to seek legal advice is as soon as they think there may be a problem and before they have responded to it.

Anyone who has read Sebastian *Junger's A Perfect Storm*, or seen the movie, understands that fishermen earn their living by hard work in the face of great danger. There was a fisherman who worked on the open ocean. If his engine failed, he and his crew were in mortal danger. Soon after an engine change, the engine gave trouble, for reasons that were not clear. He was on the beach, with no income, until he could repair or replace the defective engine. He decided that the cause was a defective part that had just been installed. He contacted the supplier, and, after some toing and froing, they offered to contribute a five-figure sum toward repairs. The company made it clear that this payment came without any admission of liability. The fisherman was not satisfied and pursued them for a bigger settlement. Eventually, the company came into possession of information that caused them to withdraw their offer.

In another case, the owner of a small factory fell into a dispute with the supplier of a piece of machinery that had failed. It wasn't clear whether the cause of the failure was a defective product or an error in operating the machine. The supplier offered a meaningful amount to settle the claim. The owner scented blood. He declined to accept the settlement and became so demanding that the supplier withdrew its offer and said that the client could chase them for the money. I suspect that the language was harsh and intemperate on both sides.

In each of these cases, the clients failed to take advice until it was too late. In both cases, the client presented the lawyer with a problem that could only be solved by expensive litigation, with no guarantee of a win. The moral of these stories is that clients should take advice at the earliest possible stage and you should encourage them to do so. This is one of the reasons that I provide initial advice at half my usual hourly rate.

CHAPTER 17: LAWYERS

Some lawyers fearlessly represent their clients, yet manage to be agreeable, ethical, and reliable. Some do not, and they will be the bane of your life. They can be pompous, rude, overbearing, and unhelpful, even when that gets in the way of a speedy resolution. Law is a competitive business, and there will always be lawyers who are keen to criticise the skills and fees of their competitors.

Some lawyers always seem to have difficult clients. If you mention it to them they will always say that their clients instructed them to be difficult, but if one lawyer consistently has more than the average number of such clients it is safe to assume that the lawyer bears some responsibility for the difficulties.

A lawyer who knew little about another lawyer's case told the client that it could be sorted for $2000. The client was outraged when the bill was for $5,000, and they complained. When the dust settled, the client accepted that $5,000 was a fair and reasonable fee. The irresponsible comment caused much stress and wasted time (for the client as much as for the lawyer). If you have not read the file, you must not give advice on the matter.

Sometimes excessive stress causes a lawyer to, what the Australian's call, 'spit the dummy.' Once upon a time, there was a property lawyer who was having a bad day. He answered the phone for the 30th time, or perhaps the 50th. It was his most demanding client. He politely answered the enquiry, slammed the phone down and, in one sweeping movement, ripped the phone off the wall, and threw it through a closed window. You will learn to understand how he felt, and how satisfying it was. But there are infinitely better ways to react to stress and to manage it before you boil over.

In rugby football, a hospital pass is one which gives the ball to a teammate, just as a large player bears down for the tackle. In the law, the term is used to describe occasions where lawyers see that a case is a no-win proposition, and the file is handed to a colleague, without disclosing what is about to happen. The colleague is faced with solving a problem he or she has not created.

Early one morning, I received a phone call from a colleague who said that he was about to file a civil claim in the court but had been called away. The papers were on his desk, could I check and file them? I agreed, only to find that critical information was missing, and it would be impossible to finalise them without extensive research. My friend had realised he did not know how to do what he promised to do and decided I should take the blame. I spent a day on the case, did what could be done, and rendered a bill for about half the time engaged. The bill was not paid. My friend got angry when I reminded him, paid up with every show of resentment, and then complained about the amount.

One day a friend and colleague asked if I would witness a will. His client (testator) was housebound so we would have to go to his house. A person (who may or not be a lawyer) witnessing a will is not providing a legal service. There is no responsibility and no fee. Later, I was told that the testator had limited knowledge of English, and the document would have to be explained to him. This converted my role into one where I was acting for the client. Later still, my friend informed me that the will included provisions for forgiveness of debt, benefiting my friend's children, and I would have to advise the testator about its meaning and effect. This would require me to accept instructions, for no fee, in a situation where there was a clear conflict of interest. To eliminate a conflict of interest, the testator must instruct a lawyer with no connection to my friend's family. I said (honestly) that I did not have the expertise and declined to act.

The moral of those two stories is you must be ever vigilant, even lawyers you like may abuse that trust.

Lawyers have their fair share of foibles, including a particularly moralistic (when he was sober) lawyer who got drunk and bragged about the size of his penis and the number of prostitutes he had had sex with.

My pet peeve is lawyers who are arrogant and patronising to their clients and to other lawyers. Arguing your corner is necessary, talking down to someone is a mistake that does nothing to help to resolve a dispute.

A client was accused of running down a policeman with his truck. The truck was travelling slowly, and the policeman survived, and could positively identify him as the driver. There was strong evidence that the act was deliberate rather than accidental. The client arrived at my office with a new lawyer who had just been admitted to the Bar and had limited experience in practice; he asked that lawyer to take part in the discussion.

I started to take a history. This included questions about what the client said happened. 'Mr. New Lawyer' took part in the discussion, and it soon became clear that he was helping the client to concoct a story, rather than eliciting the client's version of events. I lost my temper and ordered them out of my office. The client found another lawyer, went to trial, may have lied his head off, but was convicted.

'Mr New Lawyer' had been suborning perjury. I had been guilty of discourtesy to a colleague. Overall, an unhappy story.

One day I was reflecting on the number of lawyers who were, unnecessarily, making my life difficult. I took out a sheet of paper and wrote down the names of colleagues who had been helpful, and whose company had enriched my life. I covered the page and decided that my profession was not such a bad one.

Watch out for the bad apples but be confident that you will meet competent lawyers who will become friends for life.

CHAPTER 18: PARTING OF THE WAYS

Sometimes the relationship between client and lawyer will have broken down, and it is in the best interests of both that the client instructs a new lawyer. The parting may be initiated by the lawyer or by the client.

It may not be anyone's fault but just a failure to develop a working relationship. It may be that the case has gone on so long that the client may have lost confidence in the lawyer. The client may be so demanding that you are worn out and dread every phone call or email from him or her.

If the client initiates the break-up be polite and professional and promptly make the file available. Wish the client well and tell him you are willing to take up his cause again in the future if that is what he decides what to do. If I am initiating the separation I ring up the client and politely explain why I believe a change of lawyer is necessary. I try to avoid blaming the client for the problem, and most clients will appreciate that the suggestion is a good one. They may even come back to you at some point.

Make sure the file is up to date and that it accurately records the competent and timely work you have done. Copy the file for your records. Post the file to the client's new lawyer. Write to the client, confirm what you have done, and wish him or her well.

Always send the client an invoice for all the work you have done. If you do not, he or she may take this as a sign that you know you have done nothing of value or even that you have stuffed things up

CHAPTER 19: DEAR MURDERER

Clients may or may not like the lawyer who has done everything possible to obtain an acquittal.

There was a leading criminal lawyer who was a veteran of innumerable murder trials. He had serious heart troubles and this information had been published in the newspapers. He received a letter from a client (whom he had unsuccessfully defended for murder). The letter expressed the wish that he (the lawyer) die a lingering, painful death.

'Mr Leading Criminal Lawyer' wrote back. The letter started "Dear Murderer", and described a trip to the beach, that he and his family were about to take. He described the fine summer's day, and the prime steaks and champagne. The last sentence of the letter asked the question: "What are you doing"? The murderer complained to the Law Society, which criticized the lawyer. I am sure the lawyer thought that criticism was a modest price to pay for an outstanding riposte.

Some lawyers gain and retain clients, despite a misdirected sense of humour. A client was unhappily married. On a Monday morning, he turned up at his lawyer's office without an appointment. He was clearly in a distressed state, so the lawyer saw him straight away. The story was that the client's wife arrived home, from a night carousing, and confronted the client in their bedroom. She was minus her underwear, had engaged in casual sex with more than one man, and described it all in excruciating detail. Finally, she pulled the wedding ring from her finger, threw it on to the matrimonial bed, and told her husband to "stick it up your arse".

There was a pause, then the lawyer asked, "how big is her finger"?

The client's response was "you bastard"!

The client is still married to the same wife, and he still instructs the same lawyer.

There were two lawyers who liked to party. They were invited to a party that started at 8 pm. They arrived at 4 pm and were well oiled (another antipodean expression) before the sun went down.

It so happened that one of them had bought a gorilla suit on a recent trip to the big smoke (as they say in Australia). He decided that it was such a great party that he should invite passing motorists. The party was on a side road that joined the main highway. He put on the gorilla suit, walked to the intersection, and started directing traffic to the side road. Everything went well until an old car, with an elderly female driver, appeared around the corner. The driver was transfixed by the sight of a gorilla directing traffic and froze. The gorilla's reflexes were slowed by the effects of half a bottle of fine tequila, he didn't get out of the way in time and was struck a glancing blow.

The story of his visit to the accident and emergency department of the hospital, where the blood-stained gorilla suit was cut off him, appeared in the newspapers the next day. The report did not name him, which was a pity because I am certain that the story would have brought him, clients.

You will never cease to be amazed by human nature.

Two lawyers ran a small law practice, specializing in real estate transactions. Both enjoyed a good single malt whiskey.

One of their clients was a man who fell out with all his lawyers. In character, he also fell out with these two lawyers, and one of the lawyers arrived home to find that an old and beautiful tree had been chopped down.

The lawyers retired to a quiet Bar to discuss the matter and ploughed through most of a bottle of whiskey. Eventually, it was decided to pop around to the client's place, have a cup of tea with him, and discuss options. At around 3 am they arrived at the client's house, and were invited in. A conversation took place in the hall, and the lawyers confirmed that the client had felled the tree. Seconds later, the client was thrown through his (closed) glass front door, out on to his lawn.

The client, a man who complained about even the most trivial of perceived wrongs, was satisfied that rough justice had been done and considered the dispute at an end. He was so impressed with the firm's conflict resolution skills that he continued to instruct them to act for him.

Colourful lawyers do things they should not, you may enjoy hearing about their antics, but you should not imitate them.

CHAPTER 20: GETTING PAID

If you want to help people, you must stay in practice. To stay in practice, you must get paid.

Clients don't like paying for legal services, even when the services are first class and result in a win. I am here putting to one side corporate clients are effectively paying with other people's money – creditors or shareholders. It is not enough to do good work. Within 24 hours, most clients will have lost any sense of appreciation they may have felt when they got their result. If the result is not a good one, many clients will believe that you not have earned a fee.

Even good clients don't enjoy paying, and you may get paid late, in part, or not at all.

An experienced lawyer once told me that there was a conflict of interest the moment a client walks in the door. The client wants a good result quickly, and to pay a modest fee. The lawyer hopes for a long case that will generate large fees. The right way to deal with this issue is to advise the client honestly and never encourage unnecessarily lengthy litigation.

A book could be written on how to achieve the elusive goal of getting paid, in full, every time. These are some thoughts on the subject.

I treat my practice like a retail store Each set of instructions initiates a transaction that is complete when the service has been provided and the fee has been paid. My emphasis is on individual transactions, rather than open-ended assistance to a client.

A lawyer cannot assume that the client will be loyal and generate future business.

Charge what the service is worth. Worth is a difficult concept to explain and understand. Factors in setting a fee include time engaged, urgency, importance to the client, and factual and legal complexity. A client who is unhappy with a fee will not want to talk about these factors. The best approach is to ensure that the client knows (as much as possible) what your services are costing.

Charge them as if you will never see them again, but not such that you know you will never see them again. Happy clients who speak positively about you, and who come back, are the cheapest marketing that you can do.

Decide what hourly rate you can justify, and what your fixed fees will be for simple cases. With simple cases, quote a fee for the job. A fee for the job is a fee that covers all work down to resolution. Explain that the full fee is payable if the problem is solved early. I explain that this provides me with a powerful incentive to resolve the problem as soon as I can. For example, the client may have pleaded not guilty. My fee covers work up to and including the trial if the case goes that far. If I negotiate a favourable plea Bargain, everybody wins. The client gets early resolution and a good outcome, and I receive a good fee, for a reduced number of hours engaged.

Be consistent with your charging practices, clients often compare notes on fees.

With complex cases, try to quote a fee for each stage, and insist that each fee is paid before you do further work.

Always be upfront with the client about how much the fee will be. If you can't give a firm quote, at least explain how the fee will be calculated (usually your hourly rate, multiplied by the number of hours engaged).

Explain the difference between a fee for the job, an estimate, and a quote.

Always be crystal clear about what service will be provided and that if additional services are required, the fee has to be renegotiated.

Provide a letter of engagement that precisely states the fee, or how it will be calculated, the services to be provided, and the agreement you have reached about terms of payment (how much is to be paid, and when).

Make it clear that expenses, such as court filing fees, photocopying, travel, accommodation, and similar expenses are additional to the fees. If I am going to incur big expenses, I ask that they are paid into my trust account before I incur them.

Send invoices and statements at regular intervals. That way the client always knows what the service is costing him or her, and the total he or she owes.

If it is the first time you have acted for the client, ask for security for payment in advance.

I charge half price for the first consultation and ask that it be paid at the time of the meeting. If the client can't or won't do that, it is a warning sign that you may not get paid for any of the work.

For simple cases, I ask that the fee is paid in full into my trust account before the court date.

Aim to get paid 100% of all fees paid. The next best result is to spot the non-payers early and bail out before you have wasted too much time.

Some clients don't intend to pay and use various subterfuges to avoid paying. One technique is a promise to pay, which is delayed several times so that the fee is not paid when the court date arrives. After that, the client is not motivated to pay, and never will. Learn from your experiences and become good at spotting them. If the client asks for credit, ask him or her how much they can pay now. If it is nothing, ask for a part fee soon, and long before the case can be resolved. If they miss that payment, they are probably never going to pay.

In cases where you have any doubts about the client's reliability, make it clear that you will only do the work if they fees are paid as agreed. If the client wants to pay by cheque, ask if there is money in the account. If they say yes then ask that they use internet banking and pay the money directly into your trust account. Alternatively, ask them to bring the fee to the court or office in cash, and issue a trust receipt.

I used to sue clients for (long-standing) unpaid fees if I thought they could pay but would not. Now I send them the invoice and two or three-monthly reminders, and if the invoice remains unpaid, write it off and get on with paying work for reliable clients. An exception might be if the amount outstanding is large, and I believe they can pay. If they cannot pay, there is no point in following up.

I accept regular small payments if the client clearly cannot pay the agreed fee in a lump sum. Use a direct debit form signed by the client, so they cannot cancel the agreed payments.

Sometimes you will be asked to review an agreement and give a client a second opinion. An example is an agreement on the division of property after the breakdown of a marriage. If there is little time engaged, some lawyers believe that a small fee is appropriate. I don't agree. The second opinion is effectively an open-ended insurance risk, and I will not risk a large claim for a small fee. Ask for a fee that covers the hours required to review the client file and obtain a clear understanding of the case. If the client agrees, you have a fee worth having, and if the client declines, then you have only lost a small fee.

There are clients who will sue you at the drop of a hat. Ask yourself: is the fee worth the risk that he or she will sue? I know of clients who had an eight-figure civil claim. They weren't satisfied with their lawyers, services, sacked them, and then sued them. The clients went to a second firm, were not satisfied with their services, sacked and sued them, and went to a third firm. For all, I know, they are with their fourth or fifth firm.

One final point about fees. If you don't charge, the client will not value your services, and it may even arouse their suspicions. I have heard of a case where an elderly client complained about her lawyer, asserting that not charging was evidence that the lawyer knew that he was incompetent.

CHAPTER 21: FURTHER READING

These books will entertain you and help you to understand practical lawyering. Books by lawyers who practice in jurisdictions based on the English model of justice illustrate the point that the basics of lawyering are consistent, whether the lawyers are practising in the United States, England, Australia, Canada or New Zealand or many other countries.

Steiner's *An Honest Calling: The Law Practice of Abraham Lincoln* (2009); Dirck's *Lincoln the Lawyer* (2008); and Dekle's *Prairie Defender: The Murder Trials of Abraham Lincoln* (2017) are fascinating, and proof positive that the elements of good lawyering are constant over time and distance.

Mark H. McCormack's, *The Terrible Truth About Lawyers: How Lawyers Really Work and How to Deal with Them Successfully* (1987) is a readable book containing many useful insights. McCormack was a Yale Law School graduate who practised law before becoming a successful agent for high-earning sportsmen. The anecdotes he uses are mostly about the relationships between lawyers and wealthy business clients but are relevant to almost any kind of lawyering. The book was also published under the title: What They Don't Teach You at Yale Law School.

Scott Turow was an Assistant District Attorney in Chicago, and his *novel Presumed Innocent* (1987) describes how a high-profile murder was investigated, and the trial of the accused. This book is my favourite lawyer novel.

Vincent Bugliosi was a Los Angeles County Deputy District Attorney, who was successful in 105 out of 106 felony jury trials. This includes 21 out of 21 murder convictions. His *Helter Skelter* (with Curt Gentry) (1974) is his account of his successful prosecution of Charles Manson, and the others who committed the Sharon Tate-Labianca murders.

John Mortimer QC was a leading English Barrister who became a High Court judge. His skills as a novelist and screenwriter are put to good use in two memoirs: *Clinging to the Wreckage: A Part of Life* (1982) *and Murderers and Other Friends: Another Part of Life* (1995).

David Pannick QC is a leading English Barrister and legal academic, His *Advocates* (1992) and *Judges* (1987) provide useful and entertaining insights into the role of lawyers and judges.

Mike Bungay QC wrote *Bungay on Murder* (1982). The author did more than 100 murder trials and countless other criminal jury trials. Ronda Bungay's memoir *Dear Murderer* (1997) is a tale of Mike's career from the perspective of a well-informed non-lawyer.

Walking on Water: A Life in The Law (2004) by Chester Porter QC, is the autobiography of a leading Australian trial lawyer.

A. C Hanlon's *Random Recollections: Notes on a Lifetime at the Bar* (1939), Sir Vincent *Meredith's A Long Brief: Recollections of a Crown Solicitor* (1966) and Kevin *Ryan's Justice: Without Fear or Favour* (1997) are all entertaining stories by experienced criminal lawyers from New Zealand.

CHAPTER 22: WISDOM AND WIT

Presidents and judges, poets, and comedians have commented on or made fun of lawyers and the law. The aphorisms and gags are entertaining and often contain insights that are valuable. The saying is that only lawyers think like lawyers. It follows that lawyers should always try to understand what non-lawyers think about the legal profession and how it interacts with the general public.

'Discourage litigation. Persuade your neighbour to compromise whenever you can. As a peacemaker, the lawyer has a superior opportunity of being a good man. There will still be business enough...the leading rule for the lawyer, as for the man of every calling, is diligence...Extemporaneous speaking should be practised and cultivated. It is the lawyer's avenue to the public. However able and faithful he may be in other respects; people are slow to bring him business if he cannot make a speech... I love to dig up the question by the roots and hold it up and dry it before the fires of the mind.'

Abraham Lincoln (Trial lawyer and 16th President of the United States)

'Not a law firm in the entire city of New York bid for my employment as a lawyer when I earned my degree.'

'I was tremendously fortunate to be alive and a lawyer, working at a university so I had more flexible hours, when the women's movement was coming alive and when it became possible to argue successfully for a view of the equal protection clause that included women'.

Ruth Bader Ginsburg (Associate Justice of the US Supreme Court)

'The main business of a lawyer is to take the romance, the mystery, the irony, the ambiguity out of everything he touches.'

Antonin Scalia (Associate Justice of the US Supreme Court)

'Being a lawyer is not merely a vocation. It is a public trust, and each of us has an obligation to give back to our communities'.

'As a child, I wanted to be a lawyer because I thought lawyers and the law were wonderful. But they are more wonderful, I think than I had thought.'

Janet Reno (US Attorney-General)

'God works wonders now and then: Behold! A lawyer and an honest man!'

Benjamin Franklin.

'If there were no bad people, there would-be no-good lawyers.'

Charles Dickens.

'Lawyer: The only man in whom ignorance of the law is not punished.'

Ebert Hubbard.

'Lawsuit: A machine which you go into as a pig and come out of as a sausage.'

Ambrose Bierce.

'The lawyers' truth is not Truth, but consistency or a consistent expediency.'

Henry David Thoreau.

'Lawyers are men who hire out their words and anger.'

Martial.

'Woe unto you also, ye lawyers! for ye lade men with burdens grievous to be borne, and ye yourselves touch not the burdens with one of your fingers.'

Luke.

'In a body [like Congress] where there are more than one hundred talking lawyers, you can make no calculation upon the termination of any debate, and frequently the more trifling the subject the more animated and protracted the discussion'

President Franklin Pierce.

'If you can manipulate news, a judge can manipulate the law. A smart lawyer can keep a killer out of jail, a smart accountant can keep a thief from paying taxes, a smart reporter could ruin your reputation- unfairly'

Mario Cuomo.

'Make crime pay. Become a lawyer.'
Will Rogers.

'A lawyer with his briefcase can steal more than a hundred men with guns.'

Mario Puzo.

'I'm trusting in the Lord and a good lawyer.'

Oliver North.

'In the courtroom, it's where a lawyer really becomes an actor. There's a very fine line between delivering a monologue in a play and delivering a monologue to a jury. I've always felt that way - I've been in a lot of courtrooms. The best lawyers are really theatrical'

Woody Harrelson.

'Deceive not thy physician, confessor, nor lawyer.'

George Herbert.

'One of the things I was taught in law school is that I'd never be able to think the same again - that being a lawyer is something that's part of who I am as an individual now.'

Anita Hill.

'I'm not only a lawyer, I have a post-doctorate degree in federal tax law from William and Mary. I work in serious scholarship and work in the United States federal tax court. My husband and I raised five kids. We've raised 23 foster children. We've applied ourselves to education reform. We started a charter school for at-risk kids. '

Michele Bachmann.

'A good lawyer knows how to shut up when he's won his case.'

Alan Dershowitz.

'If the only way a library can offer an Internet exhibit about the New Deal is to hire a lawyer to clear the rights to every image and sound, then the copyright system is burdening creativity in a way that has never been seen before because there are no formalities. '

Lawrence Lessig.

'I have a lot of good role models in my family for things off the court - like my older sister, who's a lawyer. I don't like writing papers, but she's helped me a lot. It's nice to have an art and business background because they tie together perfectly.'

Venus Williams.

'I never had an existential moment when I asked myself what I was going to do. I always wanted to be a lawyer, and I knew exactly the kind of lawyer I wanted to be'.

Alan Dershowitz.

'The power of the lawyer is in the uncertainty of the law. '

Jeremy Bentham.

'Your attitude will go a long way in determining your success, your recognition, your reputation and your enjoyment in being a lawyer. '

Joe Jamail.

'I busted a mirror and got seven years bad luck, but my lawyer thinks he can get me five.'

Steven Wright.

'I'm a lawyer. I go for due process; I go for fairness and equity - these values mean a lot to me.'

Mohamed ElBaradei.

'In the old days, you would have one lawyer to handle everything: speeding tickets, buying a house, contracts, litigation, real estate, copyrights, leasing, entertainment, intellectual property, forensic accounting, criminal offences... the list goes on. Now, you have to have a separate lawyer for each one of those categories! '

James Belushi.

'When you're dealing with a big amount of money, you should have your own accountant and your own lawyer.'

Johnny Van Zant.

'Well, I don't know as I want a lawyer to tell me what I cannot do. I hire him to tell how to do what I want to do. '

'A man generally has two reasons for doing a thing. One that sounds good, and a real one.'

J. P. Morgan.

'A jury consists of twelve persons chosen to decide who has the better lawyer.'

Robert Frost.

'If you are a lawyer, and you want to take on easier cases, you can prosecute traffic violations or something. You'd have a very high rate of success, and you probably could sleep more easily at night. But that's not what drives me.'

Amal Clooney.

'I'm a soulless lawyer. Give me any opinion and I can argue it...As a lawyer, I could engage in killer litigation with the best of them. It was war, after all.'

Megyn Kelly.

'I gather from a lawyer that there was a rehearsal yesterday. We haven't a hope. I know the presiding judge too: I've had the misfortune to sleep with his wife. He was specially picked.'

Alphonse Karr.

'But the person who scored well on an SAT will not necessarily be the best doctor or the best lawyer or the best businessman. These tests do not measure character, leadership, creativity, perseverance.'

William Julius Wilson.

'There is no better way of exercising the imagination than the study of law. No poet ever interpreted nature as freely as a lawyer interprets the truth. '

Jean Giraudoux.

'It's every lawyer's dream to help shape the law, not just react to it.'
Alan Dershowitz.

'Experience is a dear school, but men will learn by no other"
Anon.

'There is no better way of exercising the imagination than the study of law. No poet ever interpreted nature as freely as a lawyer interprets the truth.'

Jean Giraudoux.

'Going to trial with a lawyer who considers your whole life-style a Crime in Progress is not a happy prospect.'

Hunter S. Thompson (author of Fear and Loathing in Las Vegas).

'A lawyer is never entirely comfortable with a friendly divorce, any more than a good mortician wants to finish his job and then have the patient sit up on the table'.

Jean Kerr.

'As a trial lawyer, intelligence is important only in the sense that it allows you to play the game if you will. Without it, you don't even have a ticket into the competitive arena. But beyond that, it doesn't get you very far at all'

Vincent Bugliosi (Trial lawyer and prosecutor of Charles Manson).

'A Lawyer will do anything to win a case, sometimes he will even tell the truth.'
Patrick Murray.

'Compromise is the best and cheapest lawyer.'
Robert Louis Stevenson.

'A lawyer without history or literature is a mechanic, a mere working mason; if he possesses some knowledge of these, he may venture to call himself an architect'.

Walter Scott.

'McVeigh's lawyer got him the death penalty, which, quite frankly, I could have done'.

Jon Stewart.

'I started out as a lawyer and came in laterally to Goldman Sachs. So I learned myself that life is unpredictable. That you really should, in terms of your career, try to be excellent at what you're doing. I think if you focus on your job, and you focus on being broad in the context of your job, the next jobs follow from that.'

Lloyd Blankfein.

'I'm a trained lawyer, after all, so I don't have to admit to anything'
Clive Anderson.

'What I really like about law is that it's not an endless discourse like history or philosophy. In law, there comes a point where problems have to be solved, and cases decided.'

Bernhard Schlink.

'In America, an acquittal doesn't mean you're innocent, it means you beat the rap. My clients lose even when they win.'

F. Lee Bailey (Trial lawyer and defence counsel in the My Lai massacre trial of Ernest Medina).

'Law students are trained in the case method, and to the lawyer, everything in life looks like a case.'

Edward Packard, Jr.

'The first thing we do, let's kill all the lawyers.'

William Shakespeare (Henry VI, Part 2, Act IV, Scene 2).

'A lawyer is a person who writes a 10,000-word document and calls it a "brief."'
Franz Kafka (author of The Trial).

'The minute you read something that you can't understand, you can almost be sure that it was drawn up by a lawyer.'

Will Rogers.

'In the Halls of Justice, the only justice is in the halls.'

Lenny Bruce.

'He who is his own lawyer has a fool for a client.'

Proverb.

'When you have no basis for an argument, abuse the plaintiff.'

Cicero.

'I have come to the conclusion that one useless man is called a disgrace, two men are called a law firm, and three or more become a Congress'.

John Adams, in the play "1776".

'There is never a deed so foul that something couldn't be said for the guy; that's why there are lawyers.'

Melvin Belli (Trial lawyer whose clients included: Zsa Zsa Gabor and Errol Flynn).

'Imagine the appeals, dissents and remandments, if lawyers had written 'The Ten Commandments.'

Harry Bender.

'Lawyer: A learned gentleman who rescues your estate from your enemies and keeps it himself.'

Henry Brougham.

'Lawyer: One who defends you at the risk of your pocketbook, reputation and life.'

Eugene E. Brussell.

Q: What's the difference between a catfish and a lawyer?
A: One's a slimy scum-sucking bottom-dwelling scavenger; the other is a fish.

'One day in Contract Law class, the professor asked one of his better students, "Now if you were to give someone an orange, how would you go about it?"
The student replied, "Here's an orange."
The professor was livid. "No! No! Think like a lawyer!"
The student then recited, "Okay, I'd tell him, 'I hereby give and convey to you all and singular, my estate and interests, rights, claim, title, claim and advantages of and in, said orange, together with all its rind, juice, pulp, and seeds, and all rights and advantages with full power to bite, cut, freeze and otherwise eat, the same, or

give the same away with and without the pulp, juice, rind and seeds, anything herein before or hereinafter or in any deed, or deeds, instruments of whatever nature or kind whatsoever to the contrary in anywise notwithstanding...".'

Q: What's the difference between and lawyer and God?
A: God doesn't think he's a lawyer.

A lawyer dies and goes to Heaven. "There must be some mistake," the lawyer argues. "I'm too young to die. I'm only 55." "Fifty-five?" says Saint Peter. "No, according to our calculations, you're 82." "How'd you get that?" the lawyer asks. Answers St. Peter, "We added up your time sheets."

Q: What's the difference between a good lawyer and a bad lawyer?
A: A bad lawyer can let a case drag out for several years. A good lawyer can make it last even longer.

A woman and her little girl were visiting the grave of the little girl's grandmother. On their way through the cemetery back to the car, the little girl asked, "Mummy, do they ever bury two people in the same grave?"
"Of course not, dear," replied the mother, "Why would you think that?"
"The tombstone back there said... 'Here lies a lawyer and an honest man.'"

Q: What do you call 500 lawyers at the bottom of the ocean?
A: A good start.

Santa Claus, the tooth fairy, an honest lawyer, and an old drunk are walking down the street together when they simultaneously spot a hundred-dollar bill. Who gets it? The old drunk, of course, the other three are fantasy creatures.

At a convention of biological scientists, one researcher remarks to another, "Did you know that in our lab we have switched from mice to lawyers for our experiments?" "Really?" the other replied, "Why did you switch?" "Well, for three reasons. First, we found that lawyers are far more plentiful, second, the lab assistants don't get so attached to them, and thirdly there are some things even a rat won't do."

Made in the USA
Monee, IL
04 November 2026

67352873R00036